My First ACROSTIC

ALL ABOUT ME

Creative Stars

Edited By Megan Roberts

First published in Great Britain in 2020 by:

Young Writers
Remus House
Coltsfoot Drive
Peterborough
PE2 9BF
Telephone: 01733 890066
Website: www.youngwriters.co.uk

Book Design by Ashley Janson

Softback ISBN 978-1-83928-734-3

Printed and bound in the UK by BookPrintingUK
Website: www.bookprintinguk.com
YB0431C

Dear Reader,

Dear Reader,

Welcome to a fun-filled book of acrostic poems!

Here at Young Writers, we are delighted to introduce our new poetry competition for KS1 pupils, *My First Acrostic: All About Me*. Acrostic poems are an enjoyable way to introduce pupils to the world of poetry and allow the young writer to open their imagination to a range of topics of their choice. The colourful and engaging entry forms allowed even the youngest (or most reluctant) of pupils to create a poem using the acrostic technique, and with that, encouraged them to include other literary techniques such as similes and description. Here at Young Writers we are passionate about introducing the love and art of creative writing to the next generation and we love being a part of their journey.

From pets to family, from hobbies to idols, these pupils have shaped and crafted their ideas brilliantly, showcasing their budding creativity. So, we invite you to proceed through these pages and take a glimpse into these blossoming young writers' minds. We hope you will relish these poems as much as we have.

Contents

The Poems

Seaside

S and on the beach
E ating ice cream before it melts
A crab crawls on the beach
S wimming in the sea
I see boats on the water
D igging with my bucket and spade
E xploring rock pools.

Joshua Blain Shakespeare (6)
Grendon Underwood Combined School, Grendon Underwood

Lions

L oud
I n danger
O pen plains
N asty
S link, strong, surprise.

Samuel Anthony Wayte (6)
Grendon Underwood Combined School, Grendon Underwood

Winter

I am feeling
C old
E specially on my toes.

Rory Maynard (6)
Grendon Underwood Combined School, Grendon Underwood

Valentina

V ale has three brothers
A t school, I love maths
L ive with my mummy and daddy
E veryone loves me
N ice, short, brown hair
T alk to my mummy
I love ice cream
N ice, little girl
A t school, I like English.

Valentina Harper-Albornoz (5)
Ashleworth CE Primary School, Ashleworth

Monkey

M onkey swishes on the branches
O n the tall tree, Monkey is shaking
N oisy monkeys in the jungle
K ing and cheeky
E ating bananas
Y ou should watch out for monkeys.

Rosie Grenville-Cleave (5)
Ashleworth CE Primary School, Ashleworth

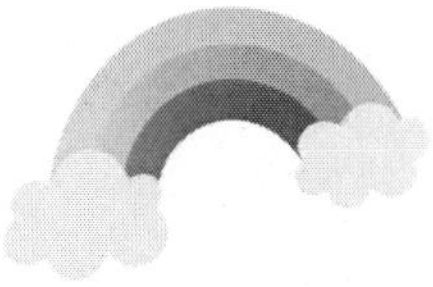

Eliska

E liska likes Lunar City
L oves to go singing
I love Christmas
S inging is the best thing I like to do
K angaroos are the best
A cake is my favourite food to eat.

Eliska Neilova (7)
Ashleworth CE Primary School, Ashleworth

Caiden

C aiden loves carnivals
A pples are my favourite fruit
I love my mummy
D rawing lovely pictures
E veryone loves me
N anny loves me.

Caiden Strachan (5)
Ashleworth CE Primary School, Ashleworth

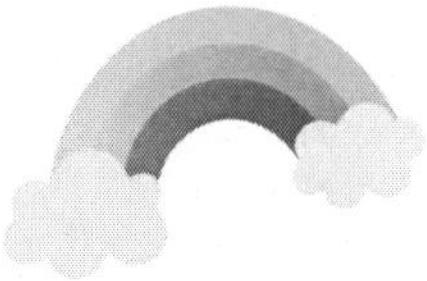

Snake

S nakes creep very carefully
N ap for a very long time
A snake creeps through the jungle
K ills a tiger
E veryone is scared of snakes.

Daniel Neil (7)
Ashleworth CE Primary School, Ashleworth

Puppy

P uppies are cute
U pside down, playing
P laying to catch the ball
P aws are pink and soft
Y ummy dog food.

Elodie Grace Anthony (5)

Ashleworth CE Primary School, Ashleworth

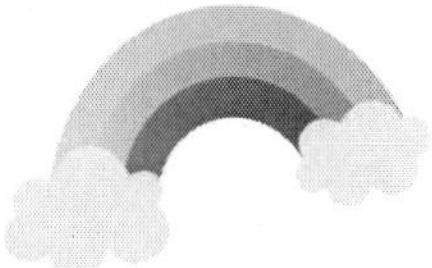

Bunny

B unnies have big ears
U p hops the bunny
N ibbles on carrots
N aps in the day
Y ou should love bunnies.

Lara Pitt (6)
Ashleworth CE Primary School, Ashleworth

Snake

S nakes slither and shed their skin
N asty bites
A ttack with teeth
K ill rabbits
E at baboons.

Freddie James Craig Pargeter (5)
Ashleworth CE Primary School, Ashleworth

Snake

S nakes swim in a river
N aps all day long
A snake slithers
K ills rabbits
E ats meat.

Dwaine Robert Evans (6)
Ashleworth CE Primary School, Ashleworth

Horse

H orses can gallop
O ats are yummy
R ide a horse to school
S it on a saddle
E at the grass.

Lottie-May Chapman-Lake (5)
Ashleworth CE Primary School, Ashleworth

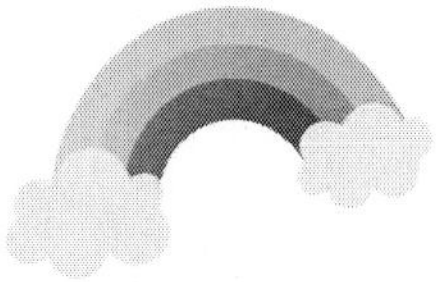

My Imagination

I could find crystals in the mud
M y pet is a unicorn with rainbow hair
A nything is edible
G ardens love water parks
I have a car that floats
N atalie eats sugar crumbs
A ll the flowers are marshmallows
T he magic round here is magnificent
I nteriors are made of melted chocolate
O ranges are made of Turkish delight
N o one flies without their wings.

Isobelle Rachel Lane (6)
Baddow Hall Infant School, Great Baddow

The Countryside

C ycling down country lanes
O ut and about, playing in the sun
U nder the bridge near the pretty river
N ice tea and cake at Papermill Loch
T ractors outside, harvesting potatoes
R abbits playing around
Y ellow sun in the sky
S unflowers in the fields
I n our cottage, the fire glows
D og walkers say hello
E veryone kicks up leaves in the woods.

Rosie Russell (6)
Baddow Hall Infant School, Great Baddow

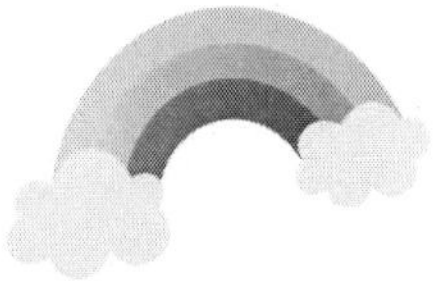

Majorettes

M arching to the music
A rms swinging to shoulder height
J umping around to the beat
O n the floor, doing my solo
R ibbons twirling round and round
E xcited for the carnival
T wirling pom-poms in our lines
T rophies waiting for us to win
E very Sunday, we like to train
S parkling leotards are the best.

Harley Galley (6)
Baddow Hall Infant School, Great Baddow

Things At The Weekend

R uby loves to do gymnastics
U nicorns are her favourite animal
B ubblegum I like to chew and blow big bubbles
Y ummy spaghetti, tomato sauce all down my chin

H elping my mum cook is so much fun
I like splashing in the water
L aughing at my dad's jokes
L ove to have sleepovers at my nanny's house.

Ruby Hill (6)
Baddow Hall Infant School, Great Baddow

Emily Ava

E ating chocolate is fun to do
M y best friend's name is Ava
I love unicorns, rainbows and butterflies too
L ucy is my sister and she is super
Y oga, running, gymnastics and swimming

A re my favourite hobbies
V ampires at Halloween and lambs in spring
A ugust is my birthday - cakes and prezzies!

Emily Brewster (6)
Baddow Hall Infant School, Great Baddow

Isabella

I am three years older than Lucia, that means I am six
S wimming is my favourite thing
A ustralia is where my daddy is from
B aby animals are what I love
E mily W and Emily R are my best friends
L ucia is my little sister who is three years old
L ewis is my cousin
A nnabel is my cousin.

Isabella Rose Whitehead (6)
Baddow Hall Infant School, Great Baddow

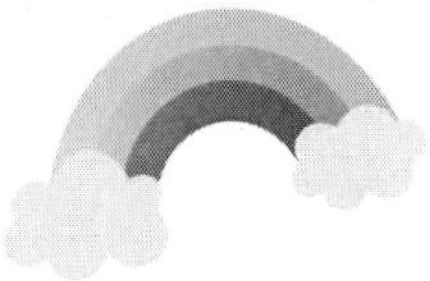

Tiger Tanks

T ough tanks
I n World War II
G ermans fighting against the British
E very soldier battling
R unning away from the bombs

T anks camouflaged in the trees
A tank gets shot by another tank
N oisy tanks that were strong
K iller tanks storming through.

Flynn Wookey (6)
Baddow Hall Infant School, Great Baddow

Animals

A lligators snap when prey goes past
N ewts silently scurry over rocks and plants
I guana is a reptile, scaly and strong
M onkey eats bananas and swings in trees
A dog is my favourite of all
L ions roar and prowl about
S cales, skin, fur or feathers.

Keira (6)

Baddow Hall Infant School, Great Baddow

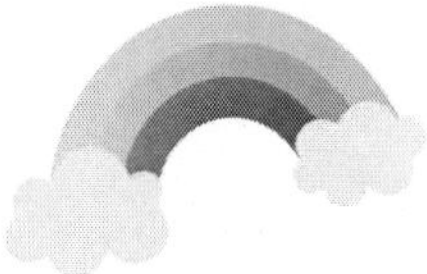

I Love Unicorns

U nicorns flying through the air
N ight and day, unicorns are working
I would love a unicorn for a pet
C ould I even get one?
O r maybe I could go to Unicorn Land
instead
R ainbow unicorns glimmer in the night
N othing is more magical than unicorns.

Kate Camryn Urwin (6)
Baddow Hall Infant School, Great Baddow

Unicorn

U p in the sky, there's a star
N ice colours like a rainbow
I love the way they say
C *lippity-clap*, we are flying
O ver the rainbow we go
R ound and round the clouds
N icely I dream about the blue sky.

Ruby Buck (6)
Baddow Hall Infant School, Great Baddow

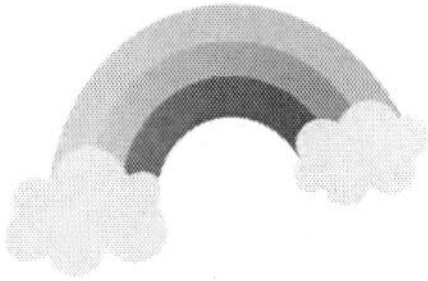

Animals

A nimals come in all shapes and sizes
N anny has two cats
I have one cat
M y cat is called Missy
A lligators like water
L ions roar loudly
S ome animals eat meat and other animals
only eat plants.

Emily Louise Russell (6)
Baddow Hall Infant School, Great Baddow

Karate

K icking high and kicking low
A t karate, we love to go
R oundhouse kicks are hard to master
A lot of hard work is what the sensei is
after
T ime and skill will help me balance
E very day is a new challenge.

William Appleton (7)
Baddow Hall Infant School, Great Baddow

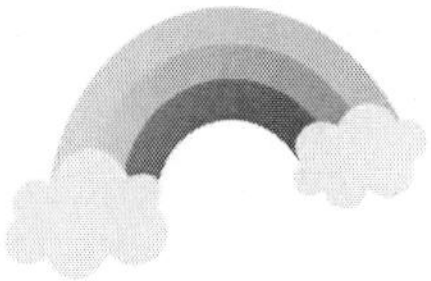

Friends

F riends are funny and make me smile
R eally cheeky too
I love my friends
E very day, we have fun
N ice and kind to everyone
D o you want to be my friend?
S ay yes because I want another friend!

Indie-Mae Lawrence (6)
Baddow Hall Infant School, Great Baddow

My Favourite Pet Animal

R abbits are my favourite animal
A rabbit jumps high
B ouncing up and down
B urrowing underground
I t loves to eat carrots
T hey chew with their four front teeth.

Tea de Merralls (6)
Baddow Hall Infant School, Great Baddow

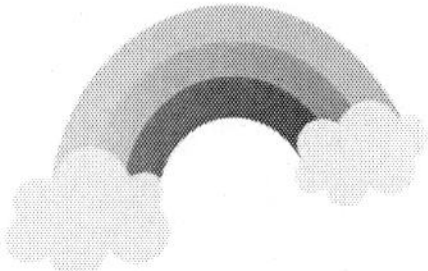

Ethan

E njoys eating chocolate
T alks a lot
H appy, I like making people laugh like clowns
A rt, I love drawing
N oisy, I enjoy pretending I'm in a rock band.

Ethan Hunt (6)

Baddow Hall Infant School, Great Baddow

Mummy

M y mummy is magical
U nbelievably beautiful
M akes me smile
M arshmallow cuddles
Y ummy cake-maker.

Bethany Walker (6)
Baddow Hall Infant School, Great Baddow

Boys

B oys are funny
O h so bad
Y es, they're crazy
S o very, very mad.

Henry McGuire (6)
Baddow Hall Infant School, Great Baddow

Dolphin

D addy is my best friend
O range is my favourite fruit
L ike my bike
P eter Rabbit is my favourite cartoon
H orse riding I like
I love swimming
N ight-time, I sleep at seven.

Zainab Momeny (5)

Downs Barn School, Downs Barn

Bianka

B irds are on the trees
I love dancing
A ani is my granny
N ight is scary for animals
K aliea is my friend and she likes me
A licia makes me happy when I am sad and
I love her.

Bianka Atanasova (5)
Downs Barn School, Downs Barn

Snakes

S *ss!* hiss the snakes
N eed a safe place to live in
A mazingly long like a school bus
K ill animals with their bites
E ven jump from trees
S wallow a watermelon.

Oscar Lewandowski (5)
Downs Barn School, Downs Barn

Space

S un is very hot
P lanets orbit around the sun
A steroid belt is a circle of rocks
C ircular is the way planets move
E very living thing is on Earth.

Hirsi Osman Farah (5)
Downs Barn School, Downs Barn

Parents

P at me on the back
A great friend
R aces me and plays
E very night, they hug me
N ice all the time
T alk to me
S py expert.

Sophie Harvey Sherwood (6)
Kelvinside Academy, Glasgow

Turtles

T hey are green
U nbreaking shells
R eally fast
T hey eat kelp
L ike to be friends
E ating nice sponges
S ea adventures.

Alex Chang (7)
Kelvinside Academy, Glasgow

Football

F un games
O n a goal
O n teams
T he players wear trainers
B all
A ttack
L ines
L eader.

Jorge Lopez (6)
Kelvinside Academy, Glasgow

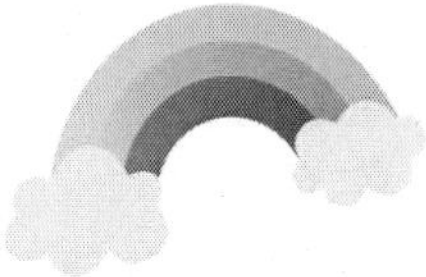

Emmett

E mmett is my name
M eeting friends
M ighty muscles
E ating food
T ucking my chair in
T aking turns.

Emmett Moreau (6)
Kelvinside Academy, Glasgow

Maple

M y dog loves balls
A pples are her favourite
P layful
L oves her food
E xpects apples all the time.

Archie Cuthbert Morrison (6)
Kelvinside Academy, Glasgow

Hector

H e is fluffy
E ars are long
C ute
T iny
O n a dog cover
R ug on a dog.

Hamish McGuigan (5)
Kelvinside Academy, Glasgow

Rugby

R unning
U p in the air
G ood for you
B all
Y ou will love it a lot.

Levon Kayes (6)
Kelvinside Academy, Glasgow

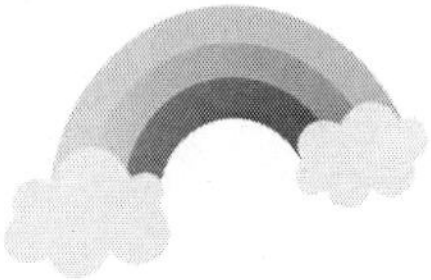

Rugby

R un
U p jumping high
G reat fun
B ig pitch
Y ou work hard.

James Mackenzie Gray Martin (6)
Kelvinside Academy, Glasgow

Dogs

D ogs can dig
O pen pink thing
G oes for a walk
S its when you ask.

Vincent Fleming-Brown (6)
Kelvinside Academy, Glasgow

Pugs

P retty
U nderground
G reat and a little bit annoying
S uper cute.

Charlie Biankin (6)
Kelvinside Academy, Glasgow

Dog

D ogs are cute
O h! My feet
G o for walks
S it on their bums.

Eve Harrison (6)
Kelvinside Academy, Glasgow

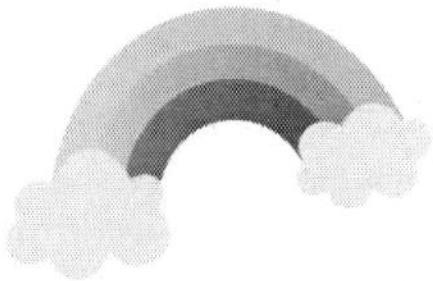

Ken

K en is my dad
E xcited when he comes home
N ice to me always.

Henry Hay (6)
Kelvinside Academy, Glasgow

Rai

R eading I love
A dventures I love
I love McDonald's.

Rai Jhund (6)
Kelvinside Academy, Glasgow

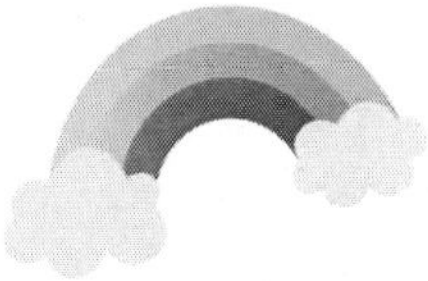

Cat

C ats are great climbers
A lways fighting
T om is my cat.

Archie Milne (6)
Kelvinside Academy, Glasgow

Pink

P retty
I nteresting
N ice
K ind.

Aubree Carr (6)
Kelvinside Academy, Glasgow

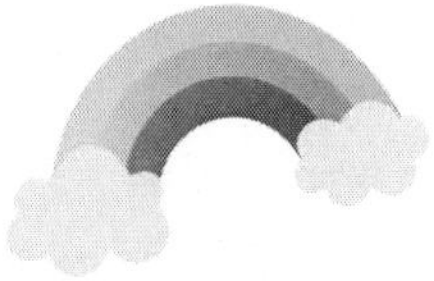

My House

M y mum is tidying the house
Y ou sleep in the attic

H ome is my favourite
O llie and I are
U pstairs and in the bedrooms
S unroom is cosy and warm
E lectric door on the garage.

Jacob Stewart (5)
Killinchy Primary School, Killinchy

My House

M y mom is cleaning my room
"**Y** our room is a mess!"

H ome is a mess
O range is the colour of my roof
U pstairs is my playroom
S miles in the house
E lla is coming.

Ella Rose Mccanny (6)
Killinchy Primary School, Killinchy

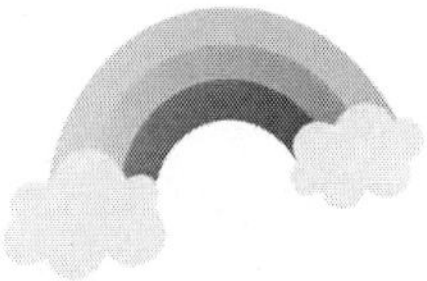

My House

M um was cross at the mess
Y o-Yo sleeps on the bed

H ouse is sold
O llie and Conrad are playing in a home
U pstairs is good
S ofia went to a hotel
E liza is my best friend.

Ailsa Rose Grindle (6)
Killinchy Primary School, Killinchy

My House

M um is cleaning the house
Y ellow on the bedroom walls

H ome is sold
O range on the walls
U p in the attic
S nakes are in the house as pets
E lectricity off in the house.

Conrad Worthy (6)
Killinchy Primary School, Killinchy

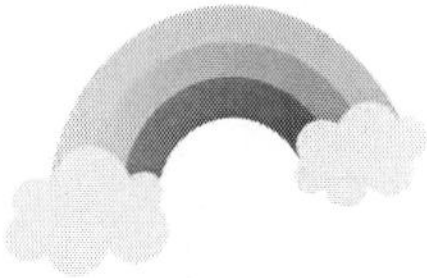

House

H ouse is new
O range is the door colour
U pstairs are three rooms
S unrooms are nice and warm
E lectricity is for the light.

Sarah Herron (6)
Killinchy Primary School, Killinchy

House

H ouse is a home
O range is the door colour
U pstairs is my bedroom
S unroom is warm
E lectricity is for the lights.

Jessica Cairns (5)
Killinchy Primary School, Killinchy

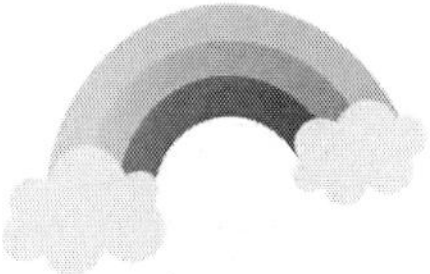

House

H ouse was cold
O utside the room was warm
U pstairs is an attic
S unroom is warm
E lectricity in every room.

Scarlett Todd (6)
Killinchy Primary School, Killinchy

House

H ome is warm
O range is the door
U p in the attic
S wimming pool in the garden
E lectricity in the bathroom.

Rhys Traynor (5)
Killinchy Primary School, Killinchy

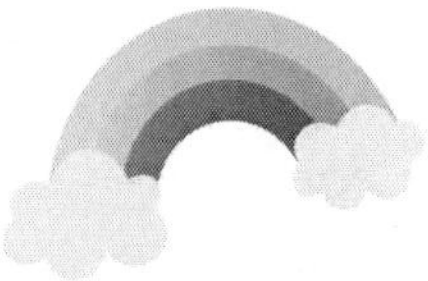

Home

H ome is warm
O n my home, there's an orange
M y mum lives in my house
E veryone sees my house.

Sarah Cheyne (5)
Killinchy Primary School, Killinchy

House

H ouse is hot
O range is the wall
U pstairs is red
S unroom
E lectricity in the lights.

Katie Watson (5)

Killinchy Primary School, Killinchy

Home

H ome is my special place
O n the road Manor Lane
M y house is fun
E veryone is always welcome.

Brodie Greenwood Black (5)
Killinchy Primary School, Killinchy

House

H ome was warm
O range door
U p the stairs
S unroom is sunny
E lectricity is on.

Isla Lynn Freya Hacking (6)
Killinchy Primary School, Killinchy

Home

H ome is cosy
O ver a hill
M y house has a fireplace
E veryone has different doors.

Luke Wilkins (5)
Killinchy Primary School, Killinchy

Home

H ome is my favourite place
O n a hill
M y family lives there
E veryone is happy.

Sofia Magowan (6)
Killinchy Primary School, Killinchy

Home

H ome is nice
O n a street
M y home is made of materials
E nd of the street.

Olivia Wijkstra (6)
Killinchy Primary School, Killinchy

Home

H ome is big
O beron lives there
M aterials like brick
E veryone is cosy.

Oberon Indio Asher Boyce (6)
Killinchy Primary School, Killinchy

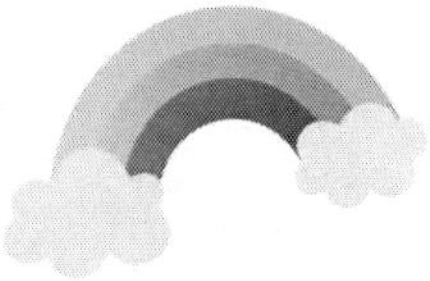

Home

H ome is on a hill
O ver the bridge
M y door is green
E veryone loves it.

Leah Trainor (6)
Killinchy Primary School, Killinchy

Home

H ome is cosy
O ver a balcony
M uck in the field
E veryone plays outside.

Felix Jamison (5)
Killinchy Primary School, Killinchy

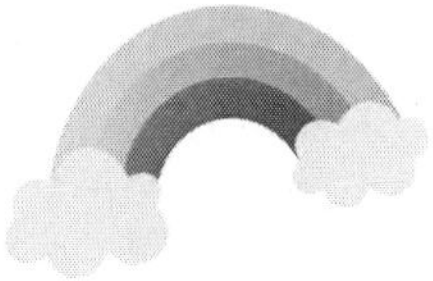

Home

H ome is comfy
O n a big hill
M y home is nice
E veryone loves my house.

Lyla Patterson (5)
Killinchy Primary School, Killinchy

Home

H ome is nice
O n a hill
M y home is cosy
E veryone looks at my house.

Faith Johnston (6)
Killinchy Primary School, Killinchy

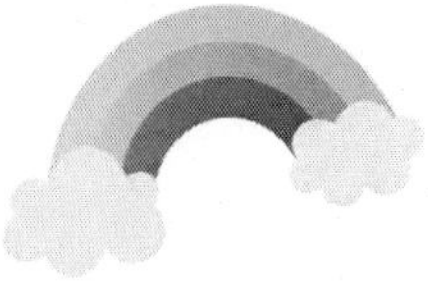

Home

H ouse is my place
O ld home
M y home is cosy
E veryone loves my home.

Ollie Brooks (5)
Killinchy Primary School, Killinchy

Home

H ome is cosy
O thers can visit
M y house
E veryone welcome.

Kate Green (5)
Killinchy Primary School, Killinchy

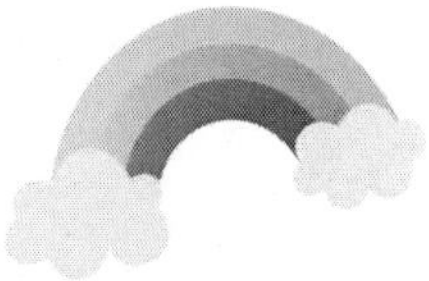

Home

H ouse number five
O range
M etal
E lectricity makes your room light.

Jack Weir (6)
Killinchy Primary School, Killinchy

Home

H ome is my favourite
O n a hill
M y house is warm
E dward likes me.

Percy Hetherington (5)
Killinchy Primary School, Killinchy

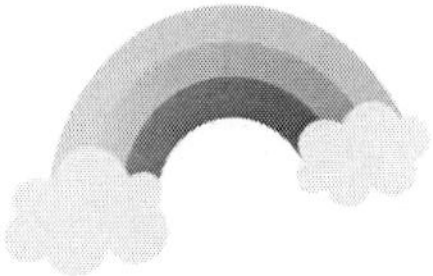

Home

H ome is hot
O n a big hill
M y home is big
E veryone likes my home.

Noah Gill (5)
Killinchy Primary School, Killinchy

Home

H ome is cosy
O n a street
M y home is good
E veryone loves my home.

Seth Plumpton (5)
Killinchy Primary School, Killinchy

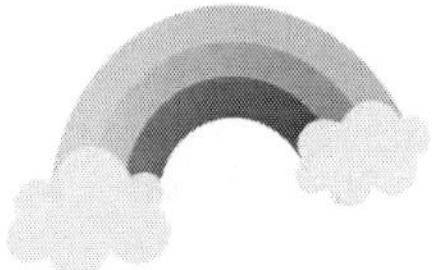

Home

H ouse is for sale
O range bathroom
M um is at home
E mpty toy box.

Erin Crooks (5) & William
Killinchy Primary School, Killinchy

Home

H ouse for sale
O range bathroom
M um is at home
E mpty toy box.

Martin Kisimov (5) & Florence
Killinchy Primary School, Killinchy

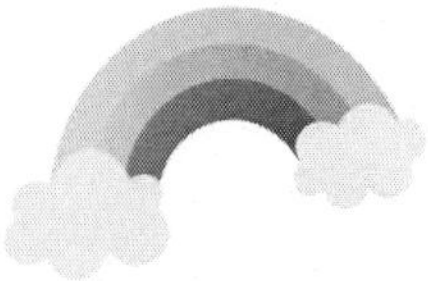

Home

H ouse for sale
O range bathroom
M um at home
E mpty toy box.

Levi McDowell (5)
Killinchy Primary School, Killinchy

Home

H ouse for sale
O range bathroom
M um is at home
E mpty box.

James Taggart (5)
Killinchy Primary School, Killinchy

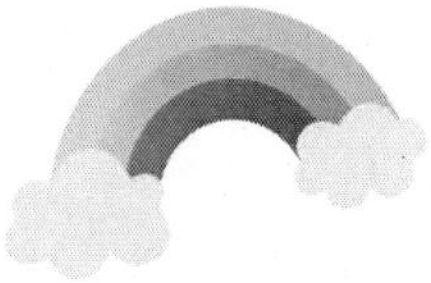

Home

H ome is cosy
O n the street
M y family
E veryone is happy.

Faith Jones (5) & Emily Gill (5)
Killinchy Primary School, Killinchy

Home

H ome is cosy
O n the street
M y family
E veryone is happy.

Mitchell Gilles (5) & Jorja Croskery (5)
Killinchy Primary School, Killinchy

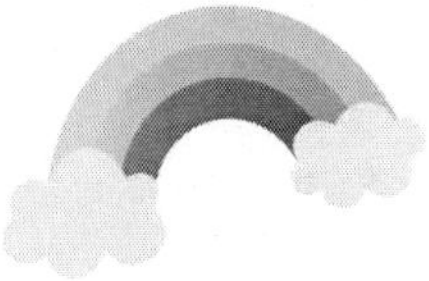

Isabella

I love cupcakes
S nakes are my favourite
A pples are my favourite
B ooks are good to read
E ggs are the best scrambled
L ove my mum
L ove my dad
A chocolate bar for a treat.

Isabella Dutton (5)
St Anthony's RC Primary School, Saltney

Martyna

M ummy is beautiful
A pples are my favourite fruit
R unning makes me fit
T omasz is my brother
Y ummy chocolate
N ice Maisie
A lways playing with my friends.

Martyna Szwaba (6)
St Anthony's RC Primary School, Saltney

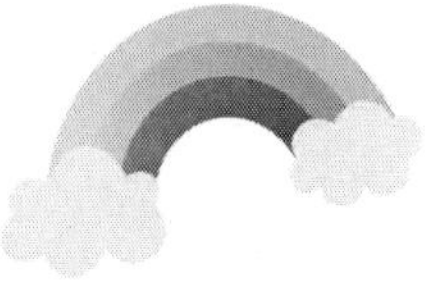

Maisie

M y best friend is Martyna
A giraffe is my favourite animal
I love my brother Isaac
S ometimes, I watch Mr Bean
I play on my iPad
E lephants have big trunks.

Maisie Gillam (6)
St Anthony's RC Primary School, Saltney

Elijah

E verybody plays football with me
L ions are my favourite animal
I love my mum
J umping on the bouncy castle
A pples are my favourite
H ave fun on Google.

Elijah Peter Fieldhouse (5)
St Anthony's RC Primary School, Saltney

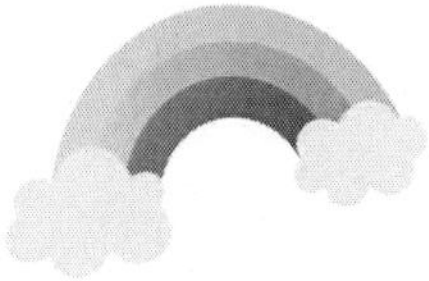

Martin

M um is the best
A pples are in a basket
R ed is my favourite colour
T igers are in the zoo
I play on my iPad
N anny lives with me.

Martin Marchesini (6)
St Anthony's RC Primary School, Saltney

Penny

P igs are my favourite animal
E ggs are my favourite food
N ew toys are the best
N anny Alison listens to me
Y ellow is my favourite colour.

Penny Brindley (6)
St Anthony's RC Primary School, Saltney

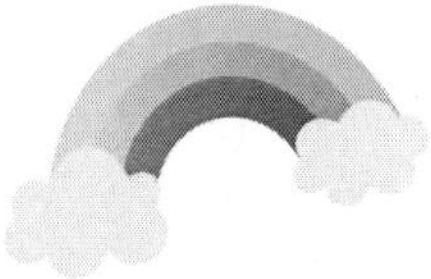

Lawson

L awson is my name
A pples are my favourite
W e go to the ice cream farm
S trawberry ice cream
O llie is my friend
N ice sweets.

Lawson-James Woods (5)

St Anthony's RC Primary School, Saltney

Torey

T eddies are good for cuddles
O nly Nan makes the best tea
R unning is my favourite sport
E xcited for Halloween
Y ellow makes me happy.

Torey-Jane Stockton (5)
St Anthony's RC Primary School, Saltney

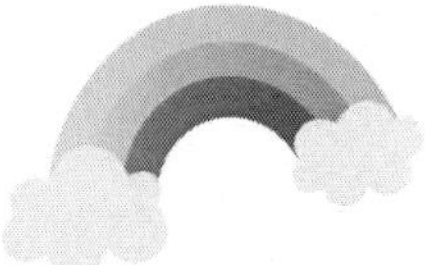

Junior

J ohn is my friend
U p in the sky
N ana
I like the sea
O ranges are good
R obots go *beep!*

Junior O'Connor (5)
St Anthony's RC Primary School, Saltney

Mylo

M inecraft is the best
Y o-yos are fun
L ast week, I played football
O ver the ramp, on my skateboard.

Mylo Michael Christopher Radford (6)

St Anthony's RC Primary School, Saltney

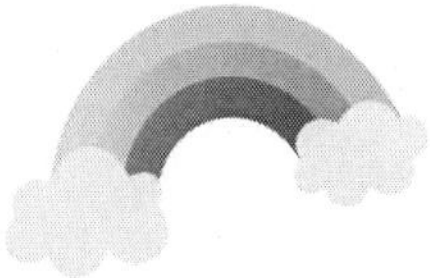

Jonny

J umping is fun
O ranges are nice
N anny loves me
N umber one is Thomas
Y ummy chocolate.

Jonny Albert Doherty (7)
St Anthony's RC Primary School, Saltney

Joe

J elly is my favourite pudding
O nly my mum can give the best hugs
E very day, I go to school.

Joseph Berry (5)

St Anthony's RC Primary School, Saltney

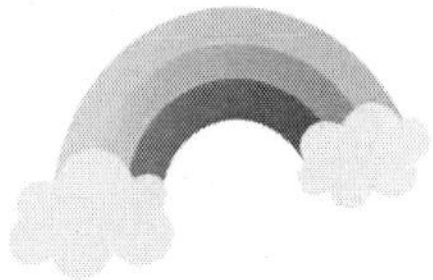

Fairy Tales

F airies are gently fluttering their elegant, beautiful wings
A ll the beautiful princesses gracefully danced on the glistening ballroom floor
I love to peacefully read these fantastic fairy-tale books
R oyal balls are held with princes waiting to meet a beautiful princess
Y ou must read the fairy tale of wonderful Cinderella

T all towers hold gorgeous princesses
A ll the wicked wizards trying to cast scary spells
L ove is seen between a stunning princess and a handsome prince
E very princess gets married to a prince
S pells are cast by wicked witches and clever wizards.

Zeynab Gafoor (6)
St Barnabas & St Paul's CE Primary School, Blackburn

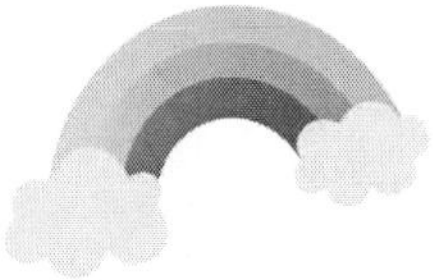

Fairy Tale

F airies are gently fluttering their elegant wings
A ll the beautiful princesses gracefully danced in the sparkling ballroom
I love to quietly read these fairy-tale books
R oyal balls are held with princes waiting to meet a beautiful princess
Y ou can read the fairy tale of wonderful Snow White

T owering towers hold flying fairies
A ll the magical wizards trying to cast a spell on the witches
L ove passes onto every princess in the world
E very prince was waiting for their princess.

Ahyaan Khalid (6)
St Barnabas & St Paul's CE Primary School, Blackburn

Stories

S pells are being cast by a mean, scary witch
T all towers contain a trapped, beautiful, kind princess with short, blonde hair
O nce upon a time, starts a fairy tale
R eading an interesting story quickly in the book corner where they have amazing work as the display and amazing books
I love to read about pretty fairies with delicate, vibrant wings
E very night, my gorgeous mum reads me my favourite stories
S chool reads us stories about mean witches and pretty princesses.

Amelia Gulzar (6)
St Barnabas & St Paul's CE Primary School, Blackburn

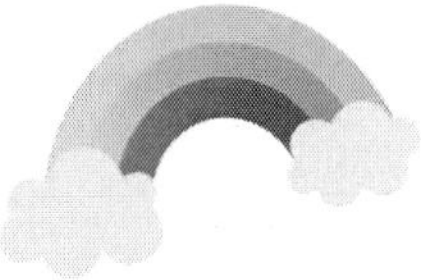

Stories

S pells are being cast by a crafty, mean witch
T all towers contain a trapped, wonderful princess with long blonde hair
O nce upon a time, starts a fascinating fairy tale
R eading an interesting story quickly in the silent book corner
I love to read about beautiful fairies with delicate wings
E very night, my kind mum reads me my favourite story
S chool reads us stories about wicked witches and princesses.

Jenna Al-Seade (6)
St Barnabas & St Paul's CE Primary School, Blackburn

School Life

S ubjects are being taught by intelligent, friendly teachers
C lassrooms that are bright and vibrant are full of hardworking children
H appy children are joyfully playing with their caring friends
O n the comfy carpet, I carefully listen to my caring teacher
O nly the best children go to my school
L unchtime gives us yummy, delicious food for energy.

Inaaya Talha (6)
St Barnabas & St Paul's CE Primary School, Blackburn

School Life

S ubjects are being taught by friendly teachers
C lassrooms that are clean are full of clever children
H ard-working children are joyfully playing with their happy friends
O n the comfy carpet, I carefully listen to my caring teacher
O nly the best children go to my school
L unchtime gives us delicious food for energy.

Maryam Ahmed (6) & Tanzeen
St Barnabas & St Paul's CE Primary School, Blackburn

Wintertime

W arm, cosy scarf and gloves
I cy, slippy roads that are abandoned
N o sun, only freezing, crunchy snow
T rees are bare from losing their dry leaves
E veryone is enjoying delicious hot chocolate
R eady for an exciting Christmas full of presents and love.

Arian Khan (6), Wasif & Leah
St Barnabas & St Paul's CE Primary School, Blackburn

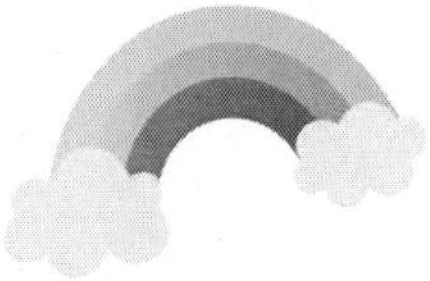

Family Life

F antastic memories with my family
A unties and uncles are amazing
M ums looking after their caring children
I n my warm, cosy, loving home
L ook at the laughter on my siblings' faces
Y ou should always take care of your
beautiful family.

Zehra Yasir (6), Ayat & Rukhsana
St Barnabas & St Paul's CE Primary School, Blackburn

Hamsters

H amsters are very cuddly
A nd my family likes hamsters too
M y hamster is the best hamster ever
T ea for me, not for you
S tay in my house, hamster
E very day, you are cheeky
R ode in the way
S tay here hamster, before you get lost!

Rafa Armond (7)
St Mary's CE School, Norwood Green

Fireworks

F ire in the sky
I nvisible flames
R ed fireworks in the sky
E mbarrassing to forget
W orks next to it
O range flames
R ed is bright
K ites everywhere in the sky
S ky is blue.

Isabella Rose (6)
St Mary's CE School, Norwood Green

Family

F antastic family
A large family
M emories are nice to share with your family
I t's lovely having a family
L ove your family
Y our cute auntie's three dogs.

Keziah Maqbool (6)
St Mary's CE School, Norwood Green

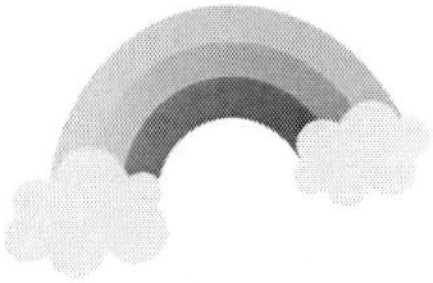

Family

F riends playing with me
A ltogether at the beach
M y family is funny and fun
I love my family
L ovely day to play all together
Y oung children play at home.

Kyrie Schutter (6)
St Mary's CE School, Norwood Green

Friend

F riendly and loving
R ude people become kind
I am nice
E xciting to have a friend
N ice to have a friend
D ark nights with a friend.

Sarah Houdaifa (6)
St Mary's CE School, Norwood Green

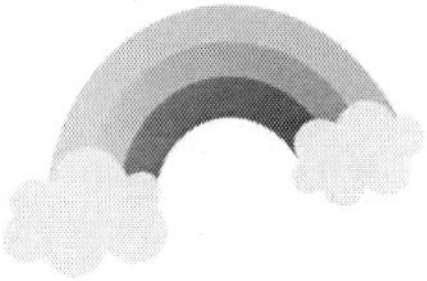

Rabbit

R ain goes in the hole
A beautiful day at the park
B eautiful, brown fur
B est bunny
I t is brown, fluffy
T oo cute, I love it!

Millie-Sophia Carter-Kapoor (7)
St Mary's CE School, Norwood Green

Hospital

H ospital sign
O peration
S py camera
P ull tissue
I see
T oilet
A mbulance
L ots of toys.

Arnav Khandekar (6)
St Mary's CE School, Norwood Green

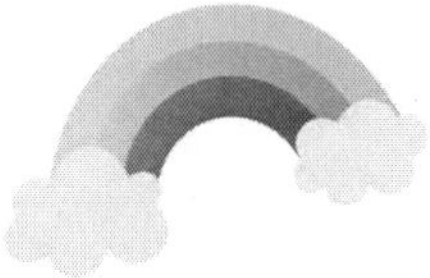

Beach

B eautiful, large beach
E xcited
A fresh, clean sea
C arpets and people lying down on the
golden sands
H appy.

Selin Hasan (6)
St Mary's CE School, Norwood Green

Alvin

A mazing
L ame friends
V iolent movies he watches
I ncredible
N osy, not good at school.

Kiy Senford (6)
St Mary's CE School, Norwood Green

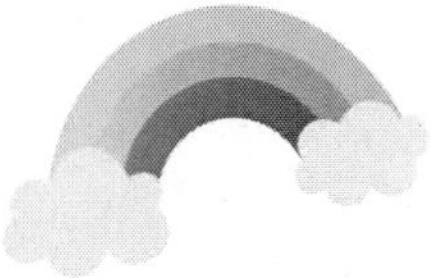

Boat

B oats go into the sea
O cean is so blue and light
A very big sunbed
T ables for people to eat on.

Anaya Kaur Dhillon (6)
St Mary's CE School, Norwood Green

Dog

D ogs are fun
O ff they go in a place
G ood Cassie.

Aryan Dhiri (6)
St Mary's CE School, Norwood Green

Explosion

E xtra dangerous lava
X iasaurus was a dinosaur, it was killed by
an explosion
P ainful magma
L ego volcanoes
O h no! Dangerous bombs
S neak gunpowder, lava is so dangerous
I ncredible extra explosion
O val volcanoes
N aughty magma comes out of volcanoes.

Oliver Ayrey (7)
St Paul's CE (VA) Primary School, Chipperfield

Reading

R ocket rhymes are sometimes in books
E xciting books are so, so fun
A mazing superheroes at the rescue
D readful adventures with Biff and Chip
I mmense characters are always waiting
for you to read them
N ever-ending stories
G reat, fun chapters.

Luke Walsh
St Paul's CE (VA) Primary School, Chipperfield

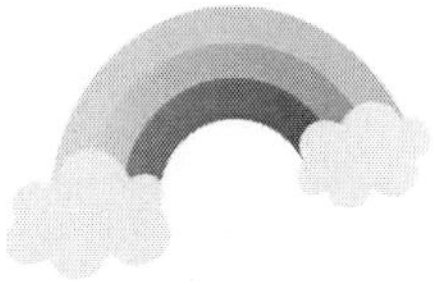

Science

S cience can be dangerous
C olourful triangular bottles in the lab
I n science, be careful
E xplosive potions that explode the building
N asty fumes make you feel sick
C hemicals make yellow, bubbly potions
E xciting experiments are very fun.

Toby Head (7)
St Paul's CE (VA) Primary School, Chipperfield

Rainbow

R ainbow sparkling in the sky
A mazing colours
I ndigo is as beautiful as a unicorn
N ature has lots of colours like a rainbow
B lue is as amazing as my bedroom
O ver the rainbow is a pot of gold
W ow! Rainbow is as pretty as a gem.

Alice Megan Leahy (6)
St Paul's CE (VA) Primary School, Chipperfield

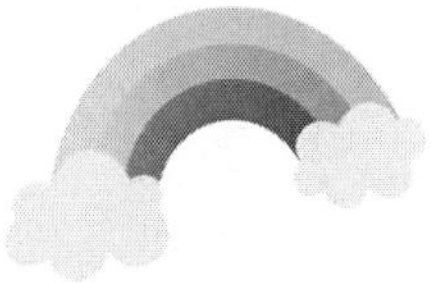

Watford

W alking into the stadium
A mazing free kicks
T hey are enjoyable to watch
F unny Harry the Hornet as the mascot
O n the pitch, they are scoring goals
R unning on the pitch like a cheetah
D eeney is a brilliant captain.

Jack Penfold (6)
St Paul's CE (VA) Primary School, Chipperfield

Roaring Like A Lion

R oaring like a lion
A ccelerating like a cheetah
C olourful race car
E xhaust fumes make you cough

C ool race cars zoom around the track
A mazing drivers going really fast
R acing to win the trophy.

Corey Fitzgerald (6)
St Paul's CE (VA) Primary School, Chipperfield

Football

F ootball is exciting
O n a team, eleven players
O h no, the other team has scored
T echnical teamwork
B all in the back of the net
A mazing teams to watch
L ovely players
L ook at their skill.

Dylan James Woolfenden (6)
St Paul's CE (VA) Primary School, Chipperfield

Rainbow

R ainy and sunny, it is beautiful
A perfect sun lights the sky
I n my house, I see a rainbow
N ight-time rainbows
B eautiful fairies on rainbows
O n a nice day
W hen there is a rainbow, I am happy.

Beth Shaw (6)
St Paul's CE (VA) Primary School, Chipperfield

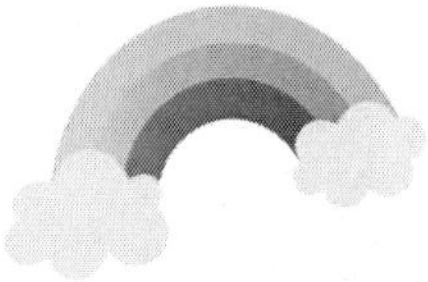

Reading

R hyming is mysterious
E njoyable as playing with my dog
A wful books, explorer books
D angling people in books
I maginative as an adventure
N avigating books
G ruesome, gorgeous adventure.

Oscar Parker (6)
St Paul's CE (VA) Primary School, Chipperfield

Crazy Camping

C razy camping
A ctivities on the river
M assive field to play in
P opping party
I ncredible camping, toasting
marshmallows by the fire
N ot a rainy day, hooray
G reat, amazing holiday.

Lui Gosling (7)
St Paul's CE (VA) Primary School, Chipperfield

Watford

W alking to the stadium
A mazing players scoring goals
T errific people scoring goals
F unny Harry the Hornet
O n fire, scoring goals
R unning to the stadium
D eeney is my favourite.

Tom Deacon (6)
St Paul's CE (VA) Primary School, Chipperfield

Kitten

K ind as a real person
I t is as fluffy as a bunny
T ough as a boxer
T iny as a cucumber
E ating tasty food all the time
N icely playing all the time.

Philippa Kenny
St Paul's CE (VA) Primary School, Chipperfield

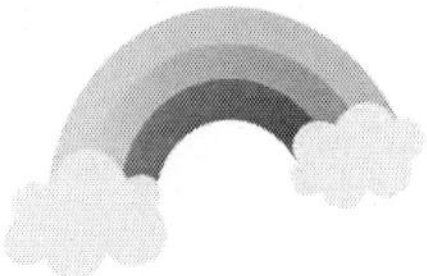

YoungWriters
Est. 1991

Young Writers Information

We hope you have enjoyed reading this book – and that you will continue to in the coming years.

If you're a young writer who enjoys reading and creative writing, or the parent of an enthusiastic poet or story writer, do visit our website **www.youngwriters.co.uk**. Here you will find free competitions, workshops and games, as well as recommended reads, a poetry glossary and our blog. There's lots to keep budding writers motivated to write!

If you would like to order further copies of this book, or any of our other titles, then please give us a call or order via your online account.

Young Writers
Remus House
Coltsfoot Drive
Peterborough
PE2 9BF
(01733) 890066
info@youngwriters.co.uk

Join in the conversation!
Tips, news, giveaways and much more!

YoungWritersUK **@YoungWritersCW**